GLADIOLA GARDEN

GLADIOLA GARDEN

POEMS OF OUTDOORS AND INDOORS
FOR SECOND GRADE READERS

BY
EFFIE LEE NEWSOME

ILLUSTRATIONS BY
LOIS MAILOU JONES

This edition published 2020
by Living Book Press

Originally published in 1944

ISBN: 978-1-922348-37-1 (paperback)
        978-1-922348-40-1 (hardback)

All rights reserved. No part of this publication may be reproduced, stored in a retrieval system, or transmitted in any other form or means – electronic, mechanical, photocopying, recording or otherwise, without the prior permission of the copyright owner and the publisher or as provided by Australian law.

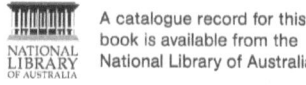

A catalogue record for this book is available from the National Library of Australia

A FOREWORD

From time to time a letter from Mrs. Newsome has come to me, always with a little poem, and from time to time I have discovered other poems of hers, in the pages of anthologies and newspapers, and always they gave me such pleasure that I was happy to learn that her verse was to be presented in a book. She has written it especially for children, but it will have charm and significance for grown-ups. The spirit of kindness, of gentle insight, and of quiet understanding underlies even the gayest of her fantasies. I feel that she makes a very real contribution, not only to verse for children but to the spirit of our time.

—Mary Hastings Bradley.

FOREWORD

When I began to introduce my children to poetry as a daily practice within our homeschool, I was struck by the homogeneity of the sweet images included within the pages of our favorite poetry books. As I read more, I heard familiar refrains and verses that struck on the many shared emotions of humanity – joy, fear, love, discomfort, belonging. But none celebrated the unique experiences of Black children and their meanderings through field and forest alongside the crickets and toads.

Feeling certain that poetry reflecting my children and their attachment to the natural world was somewhere to be found, I began a hopeful search telling myself that diligent effort would perhaps pay out in the end. And boy, did it ever.

Tucked away in the middle of a literature guide, originally published in 1941, was a passing reference to Gladiola Garden by Effie Lee Newsome with a brief description of "Poems for younger children by a Negro poet and artist." I had come to trust the guide's author, Charlemae Rollins, the head of the children's department in the first branch of the Chicago library system built in a Black neighborhood, so it was easy to follow the trail she left behind so many years ago. And sure enough, at the end of the line awaited a treasure of poems that spoke to my children, my adult sensibilities, and the little girl inside of me who had longed to see herself within the pages of a special book.

As my family soaked up the richness of Harlem Renaissance writer Effie Lee Newsome and illustrator Lois Mailou Jones, it became apparent that this volume was too plum a treasure to hold as our own. It needed to be in the home of every child – as a mirror reflecting the everyday life recognized as their own or a window giving a rare view into the playful romps and observations of brown-skinned children.

So with a thankful spirit and steadfast commitment to bring forth voices and images that will pour into the lives of so many young people, I leave you with this pot of gold at the end of the rainbow. May Gladiola Garden bless you and yours as it has me and mine.

Amber O'Neal Johnston
HeritageMom.com

CONTENTS

INSECTS AND SPIDERS

HOMES	3
INSECT FOLK	4
SWINGS	5
TWO FIREFLY SONGS	6
STRANGE	7
IN THE GRASS	9
JOHNNY GREENJACKET	10
THE HAWKMOTHS	11
SPIDER DRESS	11
THE GOLDEN GARDEN SPIDER	13
THE SWING	13
THE EARLY SWALLOWTAIL	14
BOLD VENTURERS	15
GAY CRICKETS	16
BEES	17
FIREFLY LIGHTS	17
THE SHADOW OF A BUTTERFLY	18
WHEN MISS LADYBIRD WENT TO TOWN	18
GRASSHOPPERS	19
LADYBIRDS	19
CONCERT	21
MOTHER MUD-DAUBER WASP	21

WE, THE CHILDREN

PASSAGE	25
THE PANTRY'S VIEW	26
SHAPES	27
THE QUILT	29
RED-GOLD	29
TWINS	30
CHILDREN KNOW	33
PANSYLAND	34
STRIPED TOP	35
QUOITS	35
DREAMS	36
SASSAFRAS TEA	37
CHILD'S EVENING	38
BACK	38
LOLLIPOPS	40
DOORS	41
A SONG OF HOME	41
HIDDEN PIT	43

"SPIRITUALS"	44
BAKER'S BOY	45
TO A LITTLE GOLD DAISY	46
WATCHING	47
THE RIDDLE	49

AT THE CREEK

AT THE POOL	53
THE DRAGON FLIES	55
THE CHANGE	56
CAT-TAILS	57

VEGETABLES AND FRUIT

IN THE MARKET	61
CORN HAIR	61
SAID FIVE RED APPLES ON THE GROUND	62

THE BIRDS

YOUNG BIRDS' MOUTHS	65
THE UNWRAPPING	65
MY LADY CARDINAL STEALS BLUE GRAPES	65
GOD	66
BIRD BATH	67
CHICKADEE SONGS	67
STRANGE	68
BLUEBIRD	69
KILLDEER'S SONG	69
PIGEONS	70
THE DOVE OBOE	70
PIGEONS AND PEOPLE	71
THE QUAIL AND I	73
IN ALL OTHER STUDIES THEY'D BALK	73
SONGS	73
AT THE HEDGES	74
SONG	74
CHICKADEE	75
IN BROWN AND WHITE	75
SONG	76
THE FLICKERS	77
SCARLET TRIMMING	77
THE BLUE JAY	78
THANK YOU	79
BUNTINGS	79
CHIMNEY SWIFT RUNAWAY	80

PUPPETS AND COOKIES

MISS SIMPKINS' SHOP	83
THE PUPPETS SPEAK	85
PUPPET STRINGS	86
THE WABBLY PUPPET	89
COOKY JAR BALL	92

THE FLOWERS

THE PANSIES	96
DANDELIONS	96
GOLDENROD ESCORT	98
HYDRANGEAS IN AUTUMN	98
GLOVES	98
LIVERWORTS IN WINTER	99
THE RED HONEYSUCKLES	100
WHITE CLOVER	101
THE HONEYSUCKLE VINES	101
THE MORNING GLORY	102
GAY GARDEN	103
THE HONEYSUCKLE BUSH	103
INDIAN PIPE	105
APRIL	105
MAY APPLES	105
VIOLETS	106
PANSY	107
NAMES	107
TULIP UMBRELLAS	108
THE VIOLETS	108
FLOWERS	109
CHRYSANTHEMUMS	110
JONQUIL BLOOM	110
GUESTS	111
WILD ROSES	112

SQUIRREL FOLK AND OTHERS

SQUIRREL	114
SQUIRRELS' PLAY	115
AT THE WINDOW SILL	115
GEESE	117
A TURTLE WITH A TINY HEAD	117
TURKEY	118
IN WINTER	119

THE TREES

WIND-STIRRED TREES	123

THE RIDE	123
BUDS	124
QUILTING BEE	125
CHANGE	126
"LITTLE CATS"	126
AUTUMN	126
LOMBARDY POPLAR PRINCESS	128
THE SECRET	128
THE LEAVES	129
TOWARD THE SKY	131
WRITING	132
IN WINTER	133
NORWAY SPRUCE	133

LIGHTS

THE MOUSE AND THE CANDLE	136
THE PAPER LANTERNS	138
BIRTHDAY	140
BUS LIGHTS	140

THE SKIES

SKY PICTURES	143
MOON	144
THE SKY	145
THE EXCHANGE	145
DUSK	145
BEFORE THE WHITE ROUND MOON	146
WINTER MORNING	147
ORION	147

THE SNOW, THE RAIN AND THE WIND

SNOW PRINTS	150
TRAILS	151
PRINTS	151
SNOW MAN	153
SNOWFLAKES	153
WINTER DUSK	154
THE GATHERING	154
WINTER SHADOWS	156
LIGHT	156
THE SNOW'S WAY	157
THE GAME	157
THE RAIN	159
FLAKES AND DROPS	159
SONG	159

I LIKE THE WIND	160
CAMEO	161
THE SNOW	161
TWEED	161
SNOW	162

CHRISTMAS TIME

THE MAGI CALL HIM KING	165
THE PEPPERMINT CANDY MARCH	166
THROUGH THE HOLLY WREATH	167

GLADIOLA GARDEN

In red and orange, cream and rose
The happy GLADIOLA grows
In slim green boots,
In tall green rows.
There are so many colors here,
So many tints, so much good cheer!

O little girl, O little boy,
In gardens of mixed shades, much joy,
One really has to think of you,
For you are many colors too,
In cheery dresses, suits and shoes
And those gay-colored hats you choose,
With light and gladness in your faces,
You make through earth
Gay garden places.

INSECTS AND SPIDERS

HOMES

The monarch butterfly
Is born in royal halls
With golden glints of light
Swung round the green glazed walls.

But bagworm houses, although strong,
Are crude as homes of pioneers,
And look as though they'd swung right there
From willow boughs for years and years.

It's the log cabin, I'm quite sure,
Among the moths and butterflies—
Tough silk with bits of twig stuck on,
All gray and almost of one size.

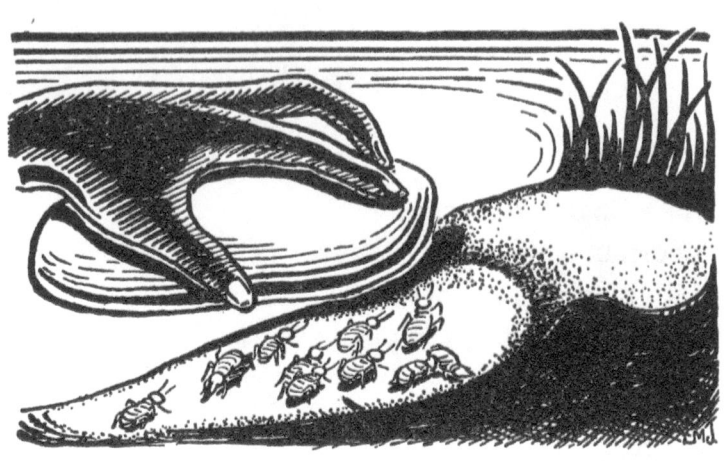

INSECT FOLK

I only have to lift a stone
Up from the soft gray ground
To start the gayest insect folk
To bustling all around.

And often when I peel the bark
From off some brown old tree
A host of small white bugs trots out
Almost immediately.

They seem to have all sorts of plans,
And everywhere to go.
And off they rush, one after one,
Like autos in a row.

SWINGS

A spider swung into the air
Upon a silver swing.
My swing is rope, and has a seat,
And out I sweep with lifted feet.
It's such an easy thing!

No easier than the spiders sway
On bits of web and float away
Much farther than my rope swing goes
All over gardens sweet with rose.

I'm certain I would like to try
Some such strange way to speed through sky.
In rope swings you just go and come
Straight back to where you started from.

TWO FIREFLY SONGS

The firefly
Goes flashing by,
A lemon-golden spark,
A dancing rhinestone in the sky,
A jewel in the dark.

Has there been some great fete today?
Here's gold confetti in night's skies,
Which darts and glows in such a way
I really think it's fireflies.

STRANGE

I never see the cricket,
But hear it every night.
I never hear the firefly,
But see its glowing light.

THE WALK

A ladybird went for a walk
Up in a great French horn,
And wandered round and round and round
Until her feet were worn.

IN THE GRASS

Sometimes I lie in meadow grass,
And watch all kinds of insects pass
In brown and red and gray.
Some very busy ants speed by
With white crumb bundles stacked up high,
All hastening in one way.

Each hurries with his heavy load
Up what I call the Cricket Road,
It looks so cool and dark.
There's pleasant millet growing there,
And wisps of fox-grass everywhere
That I use as a cane.

To push along some lazy bug,
That lags without a load to lug
Along the insect lane.
And bugs keep coming on and on—
New bands before the old have gone.
Sometimes one comes alone.

A grasshopper quick, proud and lean
Leaps to the millet, tall and green,
And takes it for his throne.

Sometimes a beetle blunders past
Or stops awhile, then starts out, fast,
As though he'd heard a call.

Sometimes a soft green worm drags by,
Then winds beneath a millet sky,
And can't be seen at all.
Each worm and bug moves on its way.
Some tap the grass, as though in play.
But I like best the ants' long string
Returning from their marketing.

JOHNNY GREENJACKET

Johnny Greenjacket, a grasshopper, gay,
Gave a great banquet one midsummer day.
The geese were all present, some quail
      and a pheasant—
This part is unpleasant—
While waiting for dinner, just after the toast,
The guests became hungry,
And ate up their host.

THE HAWKMOTHS

The hawkmoths come to evening tea
Within the honeysuckle vine.
The guests all day have been the bee.
The flowers like humming guests, I see.

SPIDER DRESS

I've seen some spiders working hard
Dressed in black velvet blouses,
Building their bridges of silk thread,
Silk highways and silk houses.
But I, when working for my mother,
Wear just some common frock or other.

THE GOLDEN GARDEN SPIDER

The golden garden spider
Has grasshoppers for lunch—
At least they hang beside her—
I've never seen her munch.
And yet they swing there every day,
And always in a different way.

Sometimes I glance at her at dawn,
But seldom find her food all gone.
It isn't hard to tell you why—
She traps grasshoppers passing by,
Then wraps them in her web all day.
When their long legs get caught they stay,
And kicking can't do any good—
Somehow, sometimes—I wish it would.

THE SWING

Little Lady Spider's built a silver swing.
Would that I were rider
On the lovely thing!

THE EARLY SWALLOWTAIL

They took their baskets piled with pears
To sell them in the market town,
And never knew that with their wares a fat, green
      larva'd cuddled down.
And as they rode, the busy thing
Spun for itself a slim, silk swing.

In town the bushel baskets stood
Banked on the market floor
Till people bought them one by one
To be sent to each door.

A little lady customer
Picks out the pears that best suit her,
And never knows her basket is
The one that holds the chrysalis.
She has it driven to her door,
And set upon her back porch floor,
Till she has canned the golden pears.
And then the basket's sent downstairs.

And there within the basement shade
The swinging chrysalis still stayed
Until the heat from furnace flame

Brought on the early change that came.
And there where not a soul could see
The thinned case opened wide,
And on a dim, cold day in March
A butterfly crawled from inside.

A butterfly all damp and strange
Came out to fan its dark wings dry.
And when the wings were large and strong
There simply was no place to fly.
For all outside the thin March snow
Swung in great scallops of wild lace.
There was no food for butterflies outdoors in any place.
The prisoner flew to the dull glass,
And could not see the gay flakes pass.
It was a time for flakes to fly,
But not for a poor butterfly.

BOLD VENTURERS

The monarch butterflies, I'm sure,
Will soon leave on their autumn tour,
They've gilded trees from day to day,
Meeting to plan their trip away.

It's all arranged quite noiselessly,
Hundreds of miles of long journey,
On trips the swallowtail tribe misses—
It stays and turns to chrysalises.

GAY CRICKETS

Without a single bit of fuss
A cricket came to live with us.
Without one little word to say
A black-dressed cricket came to stay,
And steal into a basement crack
And watch for spiders, brown and black,

And sometimes eat and sometimes play
A fiddler's tune at end of day.
It keeps up such a jolly sound,
This having crickets hiding round.
It makes the winter nights quite gay
With crickets tucked inside that way.

BEES

The bees buzz on like small brown cars,
Now that the days are sunny.
They travel on no roads at all,
Yet they arrive—how funny!

FIREFLY LIGHTS

At dull blue dusk
I've often seen
Bright fireflies flash their silver green.

And yet when skies
All glow with day
The fireflies' lights
Aren't half so gay.

THE SHADOW OF A BUTTERFLY

The shadow of a butterfly
Dropped quickly on the cement walk
And made a lovely minute-sketch,
So marvelous I could not talk.
Yet "Shadow of a butterfly"
My heart cried after it flit by,
That dainty scrap of lilac-gray
Which flecked the walk and fled away.

WHEN MISS LADYBIRD WENT TO TOWN

When Miss Ladybird went into the city
She put shellac all down her back
To make her clothes look pretty.

When Miss Ladybird went into the town
She put black spots, small polka dots,
All on her brown silk gown.

GRASSHOPPERS

Grasshoppers have great goggles on
And leap from weed to weed.
To wear such glasses just to jump
Seems what no one would need.

LADYBIRDS

Now ladybirds, you see,
Are varnished carefully,
And water doesn't hurt their stain.
I've often met them wet with rain.

CONCERT

With all in evening coats of black,
The twilight orchestra begins,
Its players scattered far and wide,
With music for the countryside.

The concert halls are every thicket.
Each player's name is just plain "Cricket."
The notes sound loud and clear and long.
And it's strong wings that make the song.

MOTHER MUD-DAUBER WASP

Mother Mud-dauber hurries all day,
Bringing wet mud for her halls,
Her funny little walls.
What will she hide inside?
Guess, if you have not tried.
The spiders she stings,
Which can't run away.
She puts them alive in her cells,
And they stay.
Then she lays an egg in each little cell,
And closes it with mud, and closes it well.
When the eggs come open on some fine day
There'll be spider dinners waiting
In the pleasantest way.

WE, THE CHILDREN

PASSAGE

My grandmother has a strange little door
That opens upon the lawn
With panels across—
I've counted them, four—
And it's just as gray as the dawn.
When Patience and I are there in the spring
We pass through this way to go violeting.
When Patience and I are out there in fall
We rush through this door
To hear the crows call.
In bright summer time beneath the blue skies,
We often steal through to find butterflies.
It has an old knocker we just love to try.
We hammer it hard each time we go by.

THE PANTRY'S VIEW

She locks the pantry door quite tight
Whenever she gets through.
But jolly little cupboard smells
Keep stealing out to you,
As though they said, "Come call some day
When that good aunt has gone away.

What need to put preserves in here,
Jellies and jams, from year to year?
It grieves a pantry very much
To hide good things no child can touch.
I wish your aunt would lose the key
That's separating you from me."

SHAPES

Yes, I watch mother hang them there—
The things I take off—on a chair.
But when she goes, and there's no light,
My clothes turn witches, every night.

THE QUILT

I have the greatest fun at night
When casement windows all are bright.
I play each window is a square
Of some great quilt up in the air,
With bits of light, and dark between,
Wherever only night is seen.

It really makes a mammoth quilt—
With blocks of black and checks of gilt—
That covers up the tired day
In such a cozy kind of way.

RED-GOLD

At night I watch the silver stars
That sparkle overhead.
In day I watch the gay goldfish
That glitter orange-red.
I often wish that in the cold
The stars would warm to reddish gold.
But, still, with gold stars overhead
I'd hardly wish to go to bed.

TWINS

We are twins. Everybody knows it—
Everybody asks it, "Are you twins?"
Soon as we go up the street,
Then the questioning begins,
"Are you little fellows twins?"

Wonder why they want to know.
Why do they keep asking so,
"Are you little fellows twins?"

And when we say, "Yes," we are twins,
They give such funny, happy grins,
As though we were the only ones.
They're Hope and Grace at Andersons',
Of course, they're girls,
But yet they're twins.

I wonder if they'll keep this up
Till we have grown to men.
I'm wondering if they'll ask right on
And on and on again,
"Say, are you twins, you two fellows?
You surely look it, goodness knows!"

CHILDREN KNOW

There are some people come to call
Who don't like children much at all.
And then still others ring the bell
Who seem to like us very well.

They like our dogs, and like our cats,
And give them little friendly pats,
And ask their names and all—
Right downstairs in the hall.

We watch them from upstairs,
Then slip down easily
When they are friends of ours
Whom we are glad to see.

Especially when they know our names
And have a lot to talk about,
Our running and our different games—
Some others just leave children out—
And all about your birthdays,
And who's the oldest now.
They're not such favorites with grown-ups,
But they suit us somehow.

PANSYLAND

O Pansyland is all the earth
When purple shadows fall,
Far more than just some tiny bed
Beside a garden wall.

All evening's dusk and gold of day
Color the skies in endless way,
And all the west is Pansyland.
We watch the colors as we stand.

STRIPED TOP

My tin top has the gayest stripes,
Yet when I spin it round
There's not one color-red nor green
Nor orange, any more, that's seen,
No stripes that can be found.
But when it stops its twirl and hum—
Then back again the colors come.

QUOITS

In wintertime I have such fun
When I play quoits with father.
I beat him almost every game.
He never seems to bother.

He looks at mother
And just smiles.
And this is strange to me,
For when he plays with grown-up folks,
He beats them, easily.

DREAMS

Sometimes I have such funny dreams
About what people said,
Or what I thought of last of all
Before I went to bed.

Way on much later in the night
They seem to tap my head,
And say, "Hello! We're back again
To talk with you in bed.

"I'm Ruby Rose, the doll you broke,
And couldn't mend again,"
Or, "I'm the naught you made too big
In printing number TEN."

Or, "I'm the dot left off the *i*,
Because you simply didn't try."
And, "I'm the little letter *b*
That you turned backward like a *d*."

And, "I'm the door that you banged to,"
Or, "I'm the skipped hole on your shoe,
To prove which fact, you'll find I bring
The very loose and unlaced string.
Perhaps I'll tie your hands quite tight
With untied shoe strings, some fine night."

SASSAFRAS TEA

The sassafras tea is red and clear
In my white china cup,
So pretty I keep peeping in
Before I drink it up.

I stir it with a silver spoon,
And sometimes I just hold
A little tea inside the spoon
Till it seems lined with gold.

It makes me happy just to smell
The steaming sassafras tea.
And that's one thing I really like
That they say's good for me.

CHILD'S EVENING

The evening seems to float along
So lightly into night,
The bird songs seem to sing to stars
To make them gay and bright.
The evening cools her lilac hair
And spreads her pink smile everywhere.

BACK

When I come back from summer camp,
"Why, how you've grown!"
They always say.
I think sometimes they must forget
My tallness when I went away.

LOLLIPOPS

How strange that all the little shops
To which I go sell lollipops!
Strange that the shops I know so well
Should all have lollipops to sell!

DOORS

I hear some doors that give a whine
Just like a kitten's sound.
And others are as still as cats
When there's a mouse around.

A SONG OF HOME

My native land, I'm glad, is here,
The fairest land on earth.
My parents bought it with their toil,
Their honor and their worth,
Bought with a wisdom and a care
That earned the price for each man's plot.
And, oh, they bought with faith the skies,
The hills and all that changes not.

HIDDEN PIT

We have a hidden pit
Deep down in our ravine.
We've buried things in it,
Rich treasure stuff, I mean.
We have silkworm cocoons,
A stone with squirrel footprints,
And then a larger stone
With funny little glints.
We have a horse's tooth,
With name all on a card.
We've got a piece of wood
That's really turning hard.
We think some day it might make coal,
Buried down deep in our big hole.
Oh, there're all kinds of things
Of which I haven't told.
We're going to use this pit
Till we are grown and old.

"SPIRITUALS"

I like to think of David's harp
With strings of shining gold,
Playing a tinkling little tune
Back in the days of old.

I know a song that tells of this,
And one of chariots.
I'd like to see them swinging low
Like weeping willows when they blow.

BAKER'S BOY

The baker's boy delivers loaves
All up and down our street.
His car is white, his clothes are white,
White to his very feet.

I wonder how he stays that way.
I don't see how he does all day.
I'd like to watch him going home,
When all the loaves are out.
His clothes must look quite different then,
At least, I have no doubt.

TO A LITTLE GOLD DAISY

Wise black-eyed Susan in the valley,
I've something you shall hear.
If you can reach up on tiptoe
I'll whisper in your ear.

I love your deep, dark gypsy eyes,
Because my own are dark.
I like your sunny, golden face,
Gay as the firefly's spark.

I like your little quiet way
Of being pleasant through the day.
And then I like your name of Sue,
Because, you see, that's my name, too.

WATCHING

They often send me to the store,
And let me go alone,
Yet peep and watch till I get back,
Just why, I've never known.

If they're afraid I might get lost,
Why do they send me then,
And look from windows and front doors
Till I get back again?
They ought to trust a child of four
To run right to the grocery store.

And when I'm back they seem surprised
To see that I have bought
The very things they sent me for—
I wonder what they thought.

When they themselves go to the store,
No one looks out to see,
Nobody ever watches then—
Excepting only me.

And I just watch grown folk because
They're always playing Santa Claus,
And when they come back from the shops
They'll bring you nuts and lollipops.

THE RIDDLE

A secret and a riddle
Are different in this way,
One you must never, never tell,
And one you tell in play.
The riddle's pleasanter to me,
For riddles set my secrets free.

AT THE CREEK

AT THE POOL

I like to stand right still awhile
Beside some forest pool.
The reeds around it smell so fresh,
The waters look so cool.
Sometimes I just hop in and wade,
And have a lot of fun,
Playing with bugs that dart across
The waters in the sun.

They lodge here at this little pool,
All sorts of bugs and things
That hop about the shady banks,
Or dart along with wings,
Or scamper on the water top
As water-skaters go,
Or strange back-swimmers upside down,
Using their legs to row,

Or the stiff, flashing dragon flies,
The shining damsel,
The clumsy, sturdy water-bugs,
The scorpions as well,
That come on top to get fresh air
From homes beneath the pool,
Where water-boatmen have their nooks,
On pebbles, as a rule.

Then all at once kingfisher comes,
That fearless, royal bird!
To him what is the dragon fly
That kept the pool life stirred,
Or water-tigers, terrible;
That murder bugs all day?
Kingfisher comes, and each of these
Would hide itself away.

He swoops and swallows what he will,
A stone-fly or a frog.
Winged things rush, frightened, through the air,
Others to hole and log.
The little pool that held them all,
I watch grow very bare.
But 'fisher knows his hide and seek—
He'll find some one somewhere.

THE DRAGON FLIES

The dragon fly is clear and sleek—
I see him dart about the creek.
I know his secret very well—
He loves the dainty damsel.
She is a smaller fly, and vain,
With wings as bright as cellophane.

They travel far and travel fast,
But always reach some pool at last.
Why should they speed away to find
A creek that's of this very kind?—

The same gray willows at the edge
And sycamores around the ledge
Holding their white arms in the sky,
With little balls that dangle down
As though they held up very high
A lady's veil with dots of brown.

THE CHANGE

The pebbles that are brown on shore
Look red, dropped in the stream.
It really is a pleasant sight
To see dull stones shine red and bright,
It's somewhat like a dream.

CAT-TAILS

I've always thought the cat-tails strange
To put on tall brown velvet hats
With people wearing summer straws.
I've never understood the cause.

    The pussy willows like fur mitts,
    The cat-tails wear brown furry caps.
    I've never seen them pull these off,
    Although they look like winter wraps.

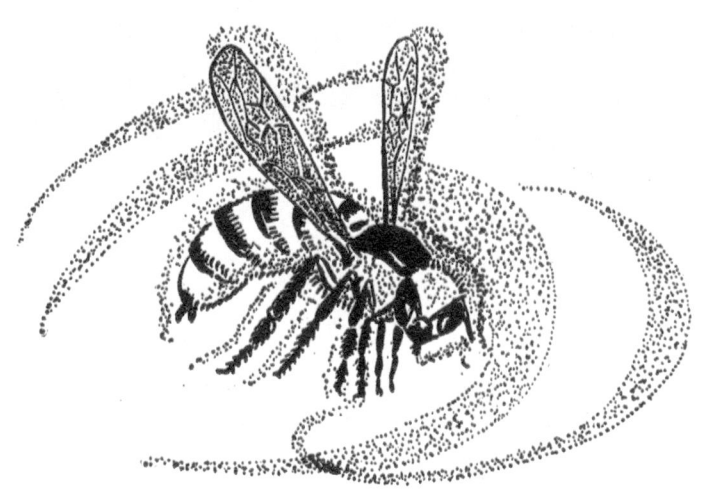

VEGETABLES AND FRUIT

IN THE MARKET

When vegetables go to the market in town
They wear the most wonderful frills on their frocks—
Broccoli and lettuce and gay Brussels sprouts
And plump country turnips in bright purple socks.

The cabbage comes wrapped in a satiny shawl,
The carrots in tight orange skirts,
Tomatoes all grinning like red country girls,
And parsley so fancy in little green curls,
Cucumbers with warts on each long, smileless face
That seems quite displeased with the town,
And beets very shabby with dull sweaters on,
Limp skirts with red streaks up and down.

CORN HAIR

The corn ear has long, silk, cool hair
That shines in goldish green.
I tear off husks and find it there,
Curled up, all fresh, and clean.

SAID FIVE RED APPLES ON THE GROUND

Said five red apples on the ground,
"Suppose we hide and don't get found!"
Sighed six green leaves upon the tree,
"Such downright selfishness, dear me!"

THE BIRDS

YOUNG BIRDS' MOUTHS

A nestful of birds' mouths
Is such a surprise.
I peeped in a nest once.
Though there were no cries,
Each bird mouth flew open—
And so did my eyes.

THE UNWRAPPING

The wintering birds look large and fat
With heavy coats of feathers.
And yet they never really sing
Till they have thinned their wraps in spring.

MY LADY CARDINAL STEALS BLUE GRAPES

My Lady Cardinal steals blue grapes!
I saw her sorrel self this day
Flit to the vines and peck at grapes.
I watched her when she went away.

I'd caught her silver, softer chirp
Answering her lord bird's deep-toned "Chuck."
I'd heard his rich song at the dawn.
Blue grapes were small pay for such luck!

GOD

Our God, who makes the many birds,
And different songs for each,
Is He who forms rough hickory bark
And smooth bark for the beech.

He makes cecropia moths so large
We wonder at their wings,
And fashions hosts of butterflies
As small as fairy things.

God gives each different nut its taste,
Each flower its own perfume,
And plants the dandelions in light,
The liverworts in gloom.

God paints so many different scenes,
Uses such changing hosts of greens,
Gives color patterns to the skies,

All day, from dawn and red sunrise.
I feel so safe to know that He
Who works these wonders cares for me.

BIRD BATH

I saw a goldfinch take a bath
Down in a forest stream.
And tiny drops like silver beads
Spattered the nearby grass and weeds.
Oh, what a rich small golden king!
Shaking such jewels from each wing!

CHICKADEE SONGS

The thickadees' spring songs I hear
Are different from their winter, notes.
How can they keep these sweet small tunes
All waiting in their little throats?

STRANGE

It makes no difference when I wake,
Some little bird has beaten me.
But who calls them before I'm up,
Has always been a mystery.

BLUEBIRD

I thought I heard
A mild bluebird
Apologizing to the breeze
For coming in among the trees
Before they'd put on their green smocks
Or taken off their white snow socks.

KILLDEER'S SONG

It pleases me to hear
The little strange killdeer.
It hurries through the sky;
And seems in passing by
To jingle little bells,
Just hosts of little bells.

PIGEONS

The pigeons find so much to eat—
I see them pecking in the street.
What is it that they relish so
That they must nibble as they go?

THE DOVE OBOE

The oboe that the doves play on
Is very soft and sweet.
I hear it in the early dawn
Across the fields of wheat.

I hear it in the dusk again
With all the skies dove-gray.
The notes, still soft, are clear and plain.
Yet what sad tunes they play!

PIGEONS AND PEOPLE

The pigeon's feet are grayish red.
Each time it steps, it jerks its head.
It jerks its head and jerks its feet,
And dodges people on the street.
And people dodge the pigeons too,
Some walking as the pigeons do,
Except nobody jerks his head.
The people swing their arms instead.

THE QUAIL AND I

At winter dusk
The quail all go
Into the twilight
White with snow.

In summer time
I hear them call
Over the millet,
Blue and tall.

IN ALL OTHER STUDIES THEY'D BALK

"Proff" Pea-green, the parrot,
Kept school in a garret
To teach other parrots to talk.
The way they learned mocking
Was something quite shocking.
In all other studies they'd balk.

SONGS

The birds must have a winter school
Where they keep up their practicing.
Each knows its song so perfectly
When they return again in spring.

AT THE HEDGES

Under the thick spruce hedges
That grow in stately row
Are catnip and wild carrot,
Quite green in spite of snow.

And high up in the hedges,
Even the dullest day,
Are merry buntings whistling
In such an airy way.

SONG

My neighbor has poinsettias
To light her winter days.
But I've red cardinals on bare boughs.
For that I give God praise.

CHICKADEE

There're going to be
For chickadee
Guests of some kind some day.
He's sharpened his beak
For fully a week.
But what's there to carve?
The poor guests will starve—
Unless there's food hidden away.

IN BROWN AND WHITE

The quail-colored fields of winter
Are wonderful sights to see,
But whether the fields
Are copying from quails,
Or quails from the fields,
Puzzles me.

SONG

A chickadee sang in the rain
A little song, "I'LL NOT COMPLAIN,"

    "I'll make my piping swift and sweet,
    Even though the notes I read are sleet,
    All written on a great ice sheet.
    My chorus still shall be,
    'Chick! Chickadee, dee-dee'."

THE FLICKERS

The flickers come to our front yard
As soon as showers stop,
And hurry round from place to place
With such a funny hop.

The flickers come in our front yard
And seem to talk together.
How can they find so much to say
In purple, misty weather?

SCARLET TRIMMING

The woodpecker folk are quite fond of bright red—
Poinsettia scarlet for neck or for head.
And whether the costume is brown, black or gray,
They count on red hats or red scarfs to make gay.
The dignified *flicker*, with linings of gold,
The black and gray *downy* that weathers the cold,
The jaunty old *red-head* in jockey outfit—
All choose blurs of scarlet to cheer up a bit.

THE BLUE JAY

The blue jay has a uniform
That seems to keep him very warm,
That seems to keep him cool also.
He wears it in the sun and snow.

THANK YOU

After I'd taken out suet and crumbs
To where the birds hide from snow
A trim chickadee
Peeped through boughs to me,
And nodded its quick head quite low,
"Yes, yes, indeed-dee,
I'm chickadee-dee,
And grateful, I want you to know.
It's kind and it's wise
To think of supplies,
For suet tastes sweet in the snow."

BUNTINGS

The dark gray buntings touched with white
Are like the fields some snowy night,
When all the snow is nearly gone,
And just small patches tip the lawn.

> I scarcely see them rushing by—
> They're speeding on, frightened and shy.
> And though they fly since I'm in sight,
> I'm startled by their very flight.

CHIMNEY SWIFT RUNAWAY

He looked like a closed umbrella
Some fairy elf had swung
With the little end turned upward—
That was the way he hung,
Clasping my curtains with all his might,
Quivering like ferns in his funny fright.

He'd dropped from his chimney nursery,
And tried to fly through
My tin kitchen flue.
I heard his wings lash,
And, quick as a flash,
I pulled off the tin
And let him fly in.

The new scenes made him quite uncertain,
That's why he held fast to the curtain
Till I'd unhooked his claws with care
And turned him free to take the air.

PUPPETS AND COOKIES

MISS SIMPKINS' SHOP

You turn one corner, then go round,
And there's Miss Simpkins' shop.
It has tin baking slides inside,
With cookies up on top.
With cookies and brown, ginger cakes
Miss Simpkins stands all day and bakes
And stacks them on a shelf,
Each kind off to itself.

I love to go and watch her make
A long legged ginger man.
She cuts her ginger men alike,
And lays them on the pan,
And you can watch them brown.
She gives each one round eyes and nose,
And there they lie in little rows.
And then you buy your favorite one,
When all the cooky men are done.

But that's not all I have to tell
About Miss Simpkins' place.
A tall young man with coal black hair
And long nosed olive face
Sits by the door in snow white hat,
White coat and trousers too,
And holds a bright green parrot up
That has a touch of blue.

The parrot walks along his arm
And gets against his cheek—
I wouldn't like that beak—
And nestles till the young man goes
To mind Miss Simpkins' cooky rows
This parrot really has its perch
That's way back in the store.
The young man takes it here to sleep—
That's what the perch is for.

And then I go on home again,
Munching my ginger man.
I'd like to keep him till I'm there.
It seems' I never can.
I eat his long legs first,
Which makes him look so bad,
I bite right on till he's all gone—
And I believe he's glad.

THE PUPPETS SPEAK

The puppets laughed about the folk
Who made them, late one night.
One claimed his joints were just a joke,
Another's arms weren't right.

One said he guessed the whole world knew
His eyes were made of laundry blue.
"I think the folk who make us
Must be themselves quite queer,"
A grandpa puppet mumbled, with something of a sneer.

A pirate puppet gave a croak,
With one hand on his belt.
He'd like to see those blundering folk,
And show them how he felt.
Why, when he finished on the stage—
He shook his wild-haired head with rage—
They hung him up, still in his swords,
And left him dangling by the cords.
A Cinderella doll declared
No one could dream just how she fared
With those step-sisters in a box,
Where none could watch them give her knocks.

The Ali Baba puppet said
He wished his bloomers weren't so red.
The Snow White puppet thought it mean
To make her have to keep so clean.
She wished her name had been Snow Gray,
Then she could tumble and be gay,
Have pleasant times when not on duty,
Instead of guarding ghastly beauty.
It truly was quite fortunate
Real folk had gone to bed.
They might have felt ashamed indeed
At what the puppets said.

PUPPET STRINGS

I heard two puppets wrangle,
With strings all in a tangle.
It seemed unfortunate that they
Should come together in this way.
For on the stage they'd bowed and vowed
And marched together gay and proud.
I guess the crossed cords made them snappy.
But maybe, though, they weren't so happy
As people thought who saw them play
In such a pleasant, smiling way.

It seems a very awkward thing—
Somebody's tangling up their string.
They can't go back upon the stage
After they've been in such a rage.

The lady's hair's torn on his coat,
His button's in her laces.
They look so wild, who could believe
Those smiles marked on their faces?

THE WABBLY PUPPET

There was a wabbly puppet
The others left alone.
Louisa'd made its head so large
It looked quite overgrown.

Some puppets moved most gracefully,
And had the love of many.
But Wabbly couldn't count his friends,
Because he hadn't any.

His head kept tumbling to one side,
And no one heard him, if he cried.
Louisa planned a puppet play,
And took the others out one day.

"You funny, rolling-headed man!
I'll put you in the garbage can."
Louisa meant what she had said,
And lifted Wabbly by the head.

She dropped him in in such a rush,
His legs were dangling out
When Sniffy, no one's little dog,
Came nosing all about,

And said, "My gentle little man,
I wish you were a steak,
Or something that a hungry dog
Could feel well paid to take.

"Still, though you're nothing I can eat,
I guess I'll drag you up the street.
I'm just a dog the others shun.
I haven't feet enough to run.

"Last winter my right foreleg froze,
So that I soon lost all my toes.
I'm always dodging in the back.
I'm never wanted by the pack."

"I'm glad to meet you," Wabbly said.
"It's just that way about my head—
I noticed that you looked surprised
To find it was so over-sized.

"Louisa scorned me every day,
Although she shaped myhead that way.
Some other puppets dress like kings.
You see I've only a mustache.
She'd planned to make me velvet things—
A tin foil sword and satin sash."

"You've moved in better groups than I."

"*You've* got a well-shaped head."

"I'm Sniffy."

"Wabbly's all my name.
If you can use me in some game—"

"I like that good idea, new brother.
We'll play that game, Friends-to-each-other."

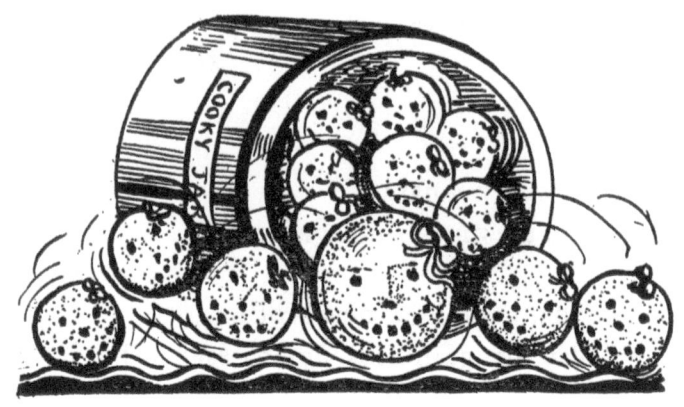

COOKY JAR BALL

"Since all the cookies here are small,
This seems the time to give a ball,"

    So declared the fat cocky in the middle of the
cooky jar, when all the other cakes were gone
but 12, 12 very small ones.

And round and round the cookies sped,
One here and there waltzed on its head.
They scarcely seemed just sweetened bread
With cocoanut for ribbon bows
And raisin eyes in rows and rows.

Of course they had no legs at all,
Yet every one enjoyed the ball,
For every single cooky tried
To dance his best upon one side.

Had I but taken off the lid—
As once upon a time I did—
And seen the cookies whirling round—
Outside I'd heard the clinking sound
Of their light taps against the wall
Of that pink jar they thought so tall!

Some careless cooky might have tumbled,
I feared, but found
That none had crumbled
Or lost their loops of cocoanut.
I feel quite sure they all forgot
That cookies weren't just baked to play
And waltz their sugared sides away,
Although one dry old cooky smiled,
"They've shut us-up! Were we so wild?
Do we seem wild? Hey diddle-diddle!
I'd dance a jig, if I weren't brittle."

THE FLOWERS

THE PANSIES

The pansies wake from winter naps
All in their fresh blue velvet caps.
I've never known how they could keep
Their hoods so lovely while they sleep.
The gold and purple look as gay
As though they'd not been tucked away
Under the earth from fall till May.

DANDELIONS

The dandelion parasols
In these strange April days
Are now umbrellas for the rain,
And then, they're, parasols again!—
To meet the bright sun's rays.

GOLDENROD ESCORT

The goldenrods in splendid plumes,
That made them all imposing,
Marched up in uniformed gold hosts
As summer's days were closing,
And led her off so gallantly,
Leaf handkerchiefs from every tree
Were cast down at her feet.
The pageant was complete.

HYDRANGEAS IN AUTUMN

Now all white scalloped caps are gone
From each hydrangea's head,
And every one wears at this time
A red-brown wig instead.

GLOVES

Wistaria's fingers in brown kid gloves
Knock now at my window-pane.
They knock in the day and they tap at night,
They rap in the wind and rain.

Last summer her bean fingers wore green gloves,
But now they're the tan of leather,
But always she taps at my casement in gloves,
Whatever the time or weather.

Sometimes she's all fringed in lavender balls
When swinging about to make her spring calls.
But whether she comes with fringe or without
She'll have on green gloves, or brown, beyond doubt.

LIVERWORTS IN WINTER

I'm sure I'll not be fooled again
By liverworts in winter time.
When I supposed they'd gone to stay
They'd only hid themselves away.

In stirring old brown foliage up—
By poking at it with one shoe
I saw the gayest, greenest leaves
Of liverworts come shining through.

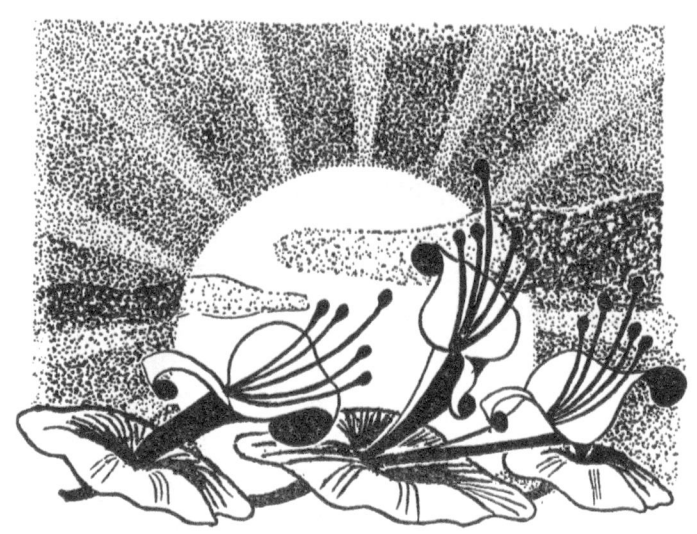

THE RED HONEYSUCKLES

When gay full summer comes at last
The trumpet honeysuckles rise,
As though they meant to blow a blast
As gorgeous as the sunset skies.

WHITE CLOVER

In their rounded snow-white caps,
Scented pleasantly,
Little clover ladies meet
In a sewing bee.

In their rounded snow-white caps,
And their great green bows,
Clover ladies meet and meet
Till the summer goes.

THE HONEYSUCKLE VINES

The honeysuckle vines are girls
Because they wear such hosts of curls
All trimmed with white and ivory bows,
So sweet they scent the wind that blows.

THE MORNING GLORY

The morning glory runs away—
I find it everywhere,
Its gay peaked sun hats upside down,
As though it didn't care.

GAY GARDEN

Your garden is so gay to me
It seems a sparkling symphony.
I think if I'd had time to stay
I might have heard your Zinnias play.

Perhaps if I'd not had to go
I could have heard your Cannas blow.
I wish I'd taken time to catch
The ringing from your marigold patch.
It grieved me much to have to go
With all your garden sounding so.

THE HONEYSUCKLE BUSH

The honeysuckle bush knows how
To bow and bow and bob and bow.
It nods when humming birds come there,
And shakes its curls of gray-green hair.
It bows at hawkmoths and at bees,
And serves some guests sweet nectar teas.
It is the gayest host of all.
From dawn to dark, winged travelers call.

INDIAN PIPE

The Indian pipe folk stand around
With white pajamas on,
And look so lazy in the gloom,
I almost hear them yawn.

APRIL

The spring's been on a month's mad march,
One wild parade from day to day.
Now that the siege is at an end,
The frightened flowers come out to play.

MAY APPLES

May apples hold green parasols,
Although they go nowhere,
And soon put snow-white sun hats on
Under their strange gold hair.

VIOLETS

The sunflowers wear great gold farm hats,
The poppies red silk hoods.
But violets wear their bowed heads bare
On highways or in woods.

PANSY

Oh, the blue, blue bloom
On the velvet cheek
Of the little pansy's face
That hides away so still and cool
In some soft garden place!
The tiger lily's orange fires,
The red lights from the rose
Aren't like the gloom on that blue cheek
Of the softest flower that glows.

NAMES

I wish the flowers' names were plain
And easy, just like Jean and Jane,
Or like flower names of pink and rose,
The kind that everybody knows.

I watch them in their little beds,
In white or gold or gorgeous reds.
I love them, pale or red like flames.
But oh! I wish they had plain names.

TULIP UMBRELLAS

Tulip umbrellas, gold and red,
Close tight when there's a shower.
That's just when people lift theirs up—
It's different with a flower.

THE VIOLETS

The violets grow in lively groups
Like ladies seated at a tea,
Their great green hats half hiding them
From visitors like you and me.

FLOWERS

The larkspur and the foxglove
Said, "Let's be cavaliers.
Salute the lady's slippers,
Those dainty little dears!"

Just then the dandelion
Came running out that way.
The larkspur and the foxglove
Nodded a quick "Good day."

CHRYSANTHEMUMS

Chrysanthemum kittens are purple and rose
With jolly green ribbons
In gay leafy bows.
They peep out from clusters,
And bounce in the breeze
Against the brown wall.·
Their little gray shadows
Go tripping like mice,
With no sound at all.

JONQUIL BLOOM

From out the jonquil's dull brown glove
Such hosts of slim green fingers rise
And lift up little handkerchiefs
Like stars in the blue skies.

GUESTS

Down underneath the whitened earth
Where none at all can see
The flowers are fixing gay spring frocks
To wear for you and me.

And some will come and bow to us
With blue sunbonnets on
Or bonnets streaked with red and gold
As gorgeous as the dawn.

And they'll bring hosts of new-leaf fans
And new-leaf parasols,
For most of them will come to make
Real full-length summer calls.
And, oh! I'm grieved when I must say
"Good-by," and watch them rush away.

WILD ROSES

Wild roses washed their bonnets out
Last evening in the dew,
And now you'll notice every one
Quite pink and fresh and new.

SQUIRREL FOLK AND OTHERS

SQUIRREL

He finds a bridge on every branch,
His trapeze is the air.
I see him leaping through all day,
And landing everywhere.
His eyes look bright each time I peep,
And yet I never see him sleep.

SQUIRRELS' PLAY

Squirrels squirm and dart, and fluff their tails,
Or let them float like little clouds.
Such jumping, joyous, sprightly things,
So filled with little leaps and springs!

They pass from airy tree-top swings
In movements very quick and neat.
It seems they hardly run on feet,
But that swift wires under ground
Were jerking each—like toys—around.

AT THE WINDOW SILL

If you pass by my window sill
You'll see a little tray.
I feed crumbs there in winter time
To birds that fly my way.

One winter night when I looked out—
Because I'd heard a sound—
I saw a flying squirrel, dim gray,
Flit swiftly toward the ground.

Though I still stared with all my might,
I only saw the silver night.

GEESE

I saw some geese go strutting by
With heads and necks held very high.
I saw six geese upon the lawn,
And each had boots of orange on.

A TURTLE WITH A TINY HEAD

A turtle with a tiny head
And little streaks of Chinese red
Came trotting gaily to the lawn
One summer day at early dawn.

I tapped him lightly with a stick.
He drew his head and legs in, quick.
Strange turtle with your streaks of red,
And folding legs and hiding head!

TURKEY

I watched the turkey's wide wings spread,
Its opened tail behind its head.
And that was all I stopped to see.
My legs rushed off quite rapidly.

IN WINTER

Sometimes they sound like little birds,
But I can tell they're only squirrels.
I see their shadows on the sill,
The purple shadows of their tails.
They dance upon my sill,
Reflected from the trees.
In winter when the leaves are gone
I like gay silhouettes like these.

THE TREES

WIND-STIRRED TREES

A tall, proud poplar's like the ocean
In tossing sound and wind-swept motion.
There's nothing more like voice of sea
Than roaring billows of a tree,
And one thinks of the foam-fringed tide
As poplar leaves wave their white side.

THE RIDE

It really is a lot of fun
To see the trees go running by.
At least, the brown-boot trunks all trot.
The green tops seem to fly.

The houses skip from place to place
And fences truly seem to race;
I'm sure there isn't anything
That stands right still in its old place.
And it's that way each time I ride—
It changes all the countryside.

BUDS

I'm rather sorry for the buds.
The spring wind shakes them so,
As though it thought that punishment
Would surely help them grow.

QUILTING BEE

Sometimes I play that in the spring
The woods get scalloped scraps of green,
And set the trees to gay quilting,
Making a merry, gorgeous scene,
A sight I like to look up to—
The sky helps piece the quilt with blue.

Then there's a change when autumn's back,
The green scraps turn to gold and red.
The dark twigs stitch them still with black,
But there're more blue scraps overhead,
And soon the whole quilt's all blue-gray—
The brighter scraps get blown away.

And now I play each empty tree
Is left there from the quilting bee.
They can't get home—so bent and old
Out there with bare hands in the cold
To wait for spring and gay green scraps
To fill their old lean hands and laps.

CHANGE

There's been the strangest kind of change
Since autumn came into the woods.
The mountain maples' summer hats
Have turned to bright red riding hoods.

"LITTLE CATS"

The catkins leap from poplar boughs
And bounce up on the roof and house
And roll and tumble on the lawn
They play like kittens on a mat.
Each one's a catkin—little cat.

AUTUMN

I hate to see the trees turn bare,
Yet, then I find nests hidden there.
I'm sad when leaves blow off in storms,
Yet glad to see the great trees' forms.

LOMBARDY POPLAR PRINCESS

Lombardy poplar princess,
So graceful, slim and tall,
You hold your proud arms upward,
Don't let them droop and sprawl,
Bending your supple body
Forward with swaying ease
Whenever strong winds shake you,
Most graceful of all trees.

THE SECRET

I used to think the trees were bare
When leaves had blown away.
But I've found hosts of buds wait there
To open some spring day.

THE LEAVES

The leaves declared, "It's not our fault
If we all turn a somersault."
The leaves said, "Winds make us act so.
They jerk us up, and off we go,
All turning over and around,
Once we've been snatched up from the ground,"
The leaves said too, "Now I declare!
It's dreadful, tumbling through the air!"

TOWARD THE SKY

The elm tree boughs grow very high,
And though I stretch up toward the sky,
They're always farther, far, than I.
But yet, as evening shadows fall,
The elm tree boughs that seemed so tall
Lie printed in a pattern, neat,
In gray-blue shadows by my feet.

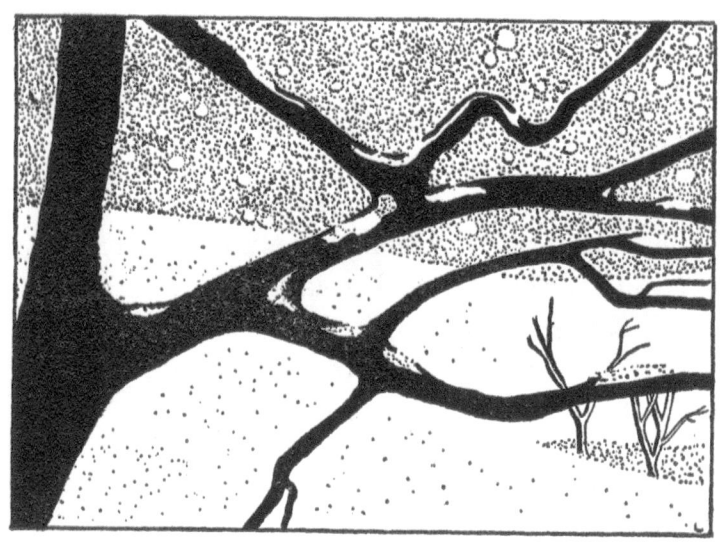

WRITING

Bare boughs look like black pencil marks
On great white books of snow.
But what the writing really is,
No one on earth would know,
With X's, V's and W's,
And loops and curves and curlicues.

IN WINTER

At winter dusk the trees all seem
To press their long, lean hands together
For company, as though they said,
"We need friends in this chilly weather.

"We hoped the fire-red west would stay
Before our bare and chilly fingers.
Its ashes everywhere are gray,
And not one red-gold glitter lingers."

The tree hands, tapering, black and bare,
With all their gold leaf jewelry gone,
Waited and watched the whole night through,
Then warmed their fingers in red dawn.

NORWAY SPRUCE

The Norway spruce has white gloves on.
Its fingers are well dressed with snow.
But when the last soft flakes are gone,
Again the rough green hands will show.

LIGHTS

THE MOUSE AND THE CANDLE

The candle seemed quite melted,
And bowed low to the mouse,
"You've come to spend the night with me,
Here in my little house?"

The mouse grew rather frightened,
And truly dropped a tear
That fell upon the candle's spark,
And left the whole room in the dark.

"Now", cried the mouse, "I'm not afraid.
It's really fortunate I stayed.
I've tasted tallow long ago.
I didn't know you with that glow.

"Your black wick tail's a stubby one.
Has it been nibbled off in fun?
I'm sure the feasting was quite gay,
Therefore, I'll eat your wax away.
And oh! your bows are so polite,
I know they'll sweeten every bite."

THE PAPER LANTERNS

The paper lanterns held a fete
When all the folks had gone to bed.
The sleepy trees were startled, late,
To notice lights of blue and red.

The maple asked the sycamore,
"Have you seen lighted fruits before?"
The sycamore breathed to the oak,
"I rather think it's just a joke."

The poplar scratched its rough old root
And groaned, "Peculiar-looking fruit.
If it's as sweet as it is gay,
I know the bees will come this way."

BIRTHDAY

The candles on my birthday cake
Kept bowing their thin heads at me
As though they said, "We're going to make
Your party joyous, just you see!"

BUS LIGHTS

The buses have red lights and green
That look like lollipops.
But candies made as large as these
Are never sold in shops.

THE SKIES

SKY PICTURES

Sometimes a great white mountain
Or snowy polar bear
Or lazy little flocks of sheep
Move on in the blue air.

The mountains tear themselves like floss,
The bears all melt away,
The little sheep will drift apart
As though they'd finished play.

And then new sheep and mountains come,
New polar bears appear,
And roll and tumble on again
Up in the skies, blue-clear.

The polar bears would like to get
Where polar bears belong.
The mountains try so hard to stand
In one place, firm and strong.

The little sheep all want to stop
And pasture in the sky.
But never can these things be done,
Although they try and try.

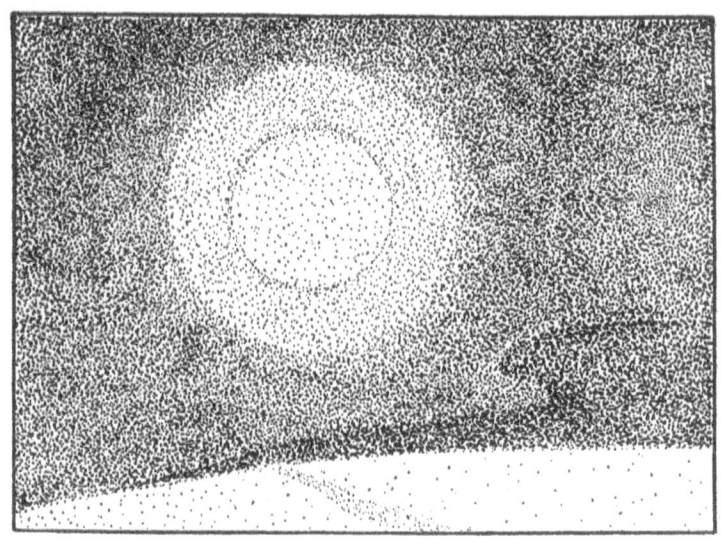

MOON

Like some cocoon wrapped soft in silk,
The dim light of the young veiled moon
Hung high up in the southern sky
Above white wastes of snow.
And there it swung, a lonesome sight,
Coddled in the cold silk of night.

THE SKY

The sky's like a beautiful, big lady's hat
That changes its feathers all day,
From snow-white to navy,
From deep gray to light,
And then to rose ribbons before the blue night.

THE EXCHANGE

When day puts dark blue night clothes on
And drops its dress of pink,
Why, who should catch it but the dawn—
Quicker than one can think?

DUSK

The evening has a noiseless way
Of wrapping up in lilac gray,
As though a lady with white hair
Drew on a shawl she'd found somewhere.

BEFORE THE WHITE ROUND MOON

Before the white round moon,
The fat clouds tumble up and down,
Each like a padded, puffy clown
That couldn't quite jump through.

WINTER MORNING

Who wrapped the moon
Like candy balls
In waxy tissue paper fold?
I saw it shortly after dawn
When all the pale south sky looked cold.

ORION

I saw Orion's silver belt
Buckled about his waist
As he went out to get that game
He's chased and chased and chased—
Just as he's done for years, I know,
Why, all my life he's hunted so.

I'm sure sky beasts are far from tame—
He hasn't yet caught any game,
Although there's plenty in the air—
Those clouds shaped like a polar bear,
And often high up in the sky
Some albatross will wander by.

THE SNOW, THE RAIN AND THE WIND

SNOW PRINTS

Along the paths my overshoes
Make little pits in twos and twos.
But often on that very day
The sunshine melts them all away.

It seems a funny kind of waste,
These footprints getting all erased.
It takes a very icy day
To ever make them really stay.

TRAILS

Grandfather never seems to know
The marks his cane makes on the snow.
Such pleasant little trails to find
By people trotting on behind.

The cane leaves holes just large enough
To drop in marbles as one goes.
So one can trace the trail right back
After the melting of the snows.

PRINTS

Wherever my dog's footprints go
There're pansy patterns in the snow.
But I'm quite sure he never knows
The petal prints made by his toes.

The five small hollows, shaded blue,
Cluster as pansy petals do.
It must be fun to trot for hours
Filling the snow with footprint flowers.

SNOW MAN

I give my snow man marble eyes,
Sometimes they're green or blue or red.
I push them in where they belong,
Up near the top of his round head.
His nose is just a small snowball.
I don't make any ears at all.
He's like no one I really know,
And yet I hate to see him go.

SNOWFLAKES

The snowflakes step so daintily
Down from a dim blue sky,
So light and joyous in their walking,
Like ladies tripping downstairs talking,
Their prancing down's such fun for all,
I can't just say that snowflakes "fall."

WINTER DUSK

The winter dusk in dainty shawl
Steps softly down and down and down,
Her white snow fringe brushes the hedge
So lightly, so slightly,
And all so very much like her
Who breathes of frozen lavender.

THE GATHERING

I saw the snow one winter day
Come flurrying in a wild ballet.
There seemed no one to play a tune,
And yet I heard the wind's bassoon.
And though the sky was dull and gray,
I've never seen a sight so gay.

The snowflake folk kept coming on
Till every tree-top seat was gone
And every spot upon the ground
Had quite filled up without a sound.
I'm sure it pleased the wild ballet
With millions coming in that way.

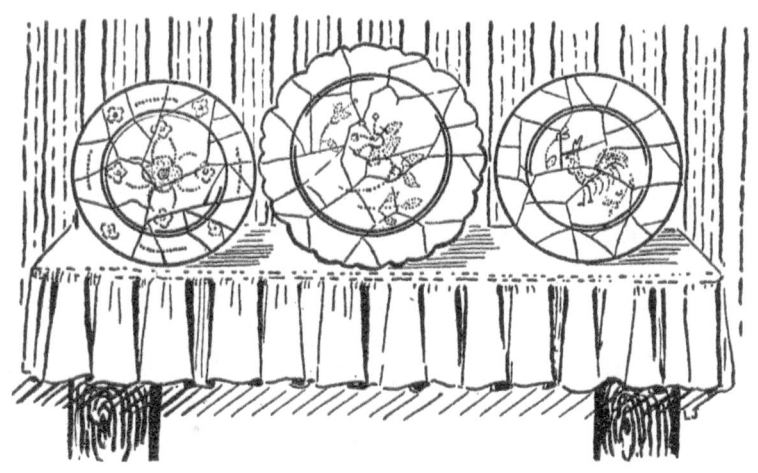

WINTER SHADOWS

Night shadows of the trees streak snow
With little twisted tracks
Like markings on grandmother's plates,
The old ones that have cracks.

LIGHT

All here and there out on the snow
The sunlight makes a sparkling glow
That seems, against the duller white,
To ring out like a bell of light.

THE SNOW'S WAY

The snow makes a blanket of wet, chilly wool,
And tries to wrap up all the trees.
But how could it think this would be comfortable,
When people with furs almost freeze?

THE GAME

I've often seen the snowflakes play
A funny little game of tag,
And dart in such a jerky way
They all get mixed up in their play.

I always find it hard to say
Which lead and which ones lag.
Their movements are so much the same
I can't find out who wins the game—
They never stop to brag.
There really seems no way to know
Who's "it," when suddenly—they go!

THE RAIN

The rain comes rustling down in silk—
I hear her coming like a queen.
I like the jewels on her dress,
The glistening of her gay necklace.
I love her tipping on the lawn,
But, oh! I'm glad when she is gone.

FLAKES AND DROPS

The snow comes down in little flakes
And rain in little drops.
The water helps to swell the lakes
And goes to moisten crops.

SONG

The raindrops tap the cement walk
As though it were a xylophone,
And play a little alto tune,
The only tune they've ever known.

I LIKE THE WIND

I like to hear the wind at night
Running along with all its might,
Over the roof and over my head,
Way up above my cozy bed.

I like to hear the wind by day,
Calling in such a jolly way,
Making my hat go sailing out,
Slapping my coat and hair about.

CAMEO

The shadows print upon the snow
A pictured purple cameo,
All set with gems, when sunshine makes
Gay jewels on the hosts of flakes.

THE SNOW

The snow's a courteous visitor.
It brings its blankets as it comes,
And goes to bed right on the ground.
It never snores nor makes a sound.

TWEED

The great snowflakes on bush and weed
Make all the world seem wrapped with tweed.

SNOW

The snowflakes fall like handkerchiefs
Down from a bluish sky,
And small winds rush up gallantly
And snatch them as they fly,
And speed like Cinderella's prince
To find the lady elf
Who dropped each dainty, lacy scrap
And win her for himself.
I've watched the winds day after day
Run with elf kerchiefs in this way.

CHRISTMAS TIME

THE MAGI CALL HIM KING

A Christmas Song

O shepherds, while you watch your flocks
The Wise Men watch His Star,
The Magi who come worshiping
With incense from afar.

Know, shepherds, you who find the place,
So humble, where He lies,
The Magi ride with splendid gifts
Under the midnight skies.

O you of sheep, who seek the fold
Of Him the angels sing,
Though He be called "Good Shepherd" too,
The Magi call Him KING.

THE PEPPERMINT CANDY MARCH

The peppermint candy march
Went gaily on up the street,
All dressed in white and red,
Each with a lime-drop head,
And bonbons like brown shoes for feet.

Each band man blew a little coil
Made of the silver wrapping foil.
I hope they got far on their way,
Because at ending of the day,
I'm sure there isn't any doubt
The hungry mice would all come out.

THROUGH THE HOLLY WREATH

I peeped once through a holly wreath.
What do you think I saw?
The round, red face of Santa Claus
With cherries in his jaw.

His nose was just a great bonbon,
His curls coconut shreds.
His lips were smiling, I could see,
In holly berry reds.

www.ingramcontent.com/pod-product-compliance
Lightning Source LLC
Chambersburg PA
CBHW020107240426
43661CB00002B/66